Discrete Categories
Forced into Coupling

—

Kathleen Fraser

APOGEE PRESS

BERKELEY, CALIFORNIA

2004

Acknowledgements

I want to express particular gratitude to my *Trastevere* writing group—
Giovanna, Donato, Arturo—whose assignments and close readings
have provided humor, committed readership and an example of steady
discipline in the years of writing this book
&
to Claire Dinsmore, whose prodigious visual talents & editing skills
have provided a visible coherence for my writing history in her on-line
journal *cauldron & net*, n.4 (Features)

EARLIER VERSIONS OF POEMS IN THIS BOOK FIRST APPEARED IN:
Common Knowledge: Soft Pages
5 FR: AD notebooks
Facture: You can hear her breathing in the photograph
    (previously titled Bernini's chisel)

INTERNET JOURNALS:
cauldron & net, n.4 (Features): Celeste & Sirius, AD notebooks
    http://www.studiocleo.com./cauldron/volume4/
Narrativity, n.3: Soft pages
    http://www.sfsu.edu/~newlit/narrativity
Titanic Operas: You can hear her breathing in the photograph
    (previously titled Bernini's chisel)
    http://jefferson.village.virginia.edu/dickinson/titanic/material/
Verdure: Celeste & Sirius, *Champs* (fields) & between, and your back
    to me inside the black suit
    http://www.acsu.buffalo.edu/~cwa/

Book design by Philip Krayna Design, Berkeley, California.
www.pkdesign.net

Cover painting "Tahiti" ©2004 by James Melchert.

ISBN 0-9744687-3-8. Library of Congress Catalog Card Number 2003114059.

Published by Apogee Press, Post Office Box 8177, Berkeley CA, 94707-8177.
www.apogeepress.com

for Irene Skolnick

Table of Contents

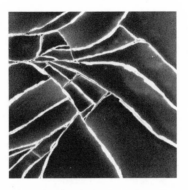

Champs (fields) & between

for Joan Mitchell, ferocity

Champs (fields) & between

1.

It was raining heavily and snowing farther up the road and she left for the appointment, both ahead of and behind her expectation, in spite of the visual impression of crashing cars and SUVs, swerving bodies in pain on the 6 o'clock news, again a swerving laid out to any random viewer, in this case herself a cinematic event to which she would gradually attach herself as she drove forward and slowly shifted gears through the lengthening

•

any random viewer, in this case

2.

You were merely setting the stage while other clients talked about the "divinely ordained" as if objects of differing colors did not slide in and out of red cells of chronic prisoners whom they were on that particular day and you knew what was commonplace and you wanted to avoid the commonplace thinking your personal uniqueness was beyond dictation, yet this fact repeated itself in his and her accounts of you as if mental anguish depended on progress or as if there were progress in the counter balance of sorrow's detail lost in the rapid intensity of its repetition

•

accounts of you   his and her accounts

3.

The air came down like rice. It scattered through unevenness and uneventfulness.

•

came down   unevenness

4.

The air came down in its teacup shape of Japanese porcelain, light dropping
through it with disturbing regularity like dry rice falling through water as if a
dream state had collaborated with the concept of "grains of rice," her observing
it at just that moment when she imagined there might be something inherent in
the weave of the curtains, that some bit of drawn thread, if pulled back, would
fold up beneath a lens coming into focus

Still the air remained full of scatterings, condensed, not exactly floating
nor promising something like the real snow she remembered as if it still existed
—morning light caught between glass slides about to be positioned beneath a
lens—grey but not heavy and less depressing because of the movement of falling

•

not exactly, beneath

5.

One felt a lift of hope beyond the opposite building's surface attached to a resin of deep amber, its sticky powder clinging to your fingers as you prepared the lengths of white horsehair attached at each end of the bow, lifting it above the stringed instrument, in this case a violin, to pull against two consonants and two vowels, their pitch—where was it?—attainable in the private ear

•

consonants   pitch—where was it?

6.

Learning to come as close as possible for two people lodged in separate bodies
to move away but without rancor re-enacting the pleasure of breaking down their
separateness, as if there were a final psychological position to grasp, to save oneself
from the other's idea of acoustic garden hose decor, stainless steel kitchen nests
& implements, glass tulips held aloft on wrought iron stems against nightfog,
emergency blink, the hovering of certain stars you'd both remembered seeing and
were counting on

•

nests & implements held aloft

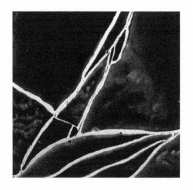

Soft pages

Soft pages

It was that motion of the back foot caught in the photo as a blur, more believable and quickly conveying a person's leaving who had once been on his way, even anticipating this place that continued to re-enter my imagination, as if the black-and-white photo of no one I knew had delivered the plot of a story it wished me to take hold of. This was not about desire or choice—the two preferred categories of explanation for my life, in conscious moments of trying to make sense (or at least an admirable clarity) of things—but about dropping into a place after that.

This was not the brass plate special: DESIRE in embossed black capitals, nameplate attached to the hallway door of apartment number 5. This was before desire, but after CHOICE.

·

Voices cutting through the air above the paper passage. Voices one can hear every afternoon at just this hour of 3:40 when certain neighbors, whose doors face Via Luigi Santini, rise out of their random snores and leave their rooms for the street and sniff the air like dogs and start barking like dogs, not knowing why they bark except the need to push one's snout at the unnatural silence and move it around. That same moment being the one in which their sharp and muffled barks have pulled me into inexplicable pleasure.

And then a siren goes off as if its car were being broken into.

·

Needing something, the cheap lined paper of those little bound notebooks imported from Germany one finds in certain shops in Rome, with cover stock of pseudo-Florentine design, somewhat faded looking, as if a businessman from Lübeck, in love with the expensive papers of Florence, but more than half in love with profit, had finally fixed upon the lepidoptera "wing-scales" pattern but had opted for its recycled version in bleached-out, cost-effective blue. I allow for that economy. A more expensive paper would dazzle you with perfection and inhibit you with its emptiness. I've found also that certain writing implements may make the difference between jumping or falling; the particular receptivity of cheap paper to soft lead or the tip of a rollerball pen can pull one into the page's porous expanse, not exactly sinking into it but not floating above it either, more like losing the sense of confine—con.fi.ne in my quasi-second language—indicating the border between two countries.

I've noticed, too, that the particular angle of my body in a certain rattan chair, purchased in Rome at one of those chain stores owned by a certain disreputable politician recently deposed, allows some entering into the liquid element. Liquidation or sequential randomness. (But I always trusted my dreams and never thought of them as abandoned film clips). One might cast off in classical terms, as in the crossing from land to water before you've noticed, which would remove an action's intentionality or at least alter it.

•

I lift the red panties with satin stripes, earlier tossed on the green radiator along with various pairs of ankle socks, among them the black cotton streaked with yellow and vermilion, still damp from the morning's rain outside in the *cortile*. Touching them. Turning them into their folds and rolling them into neat little bundles for the drawer. Some greyness begins to fall. I can see its motion sideways from the window, the graininess of newsreels from the Second World War, and I know it's more rain. No sound of voices barking, having gone in again. An animal gratitude.

By realistic representation of the foot—one woman said it was a man's foot in motion—I'm sure of that—one could be helped, technically, into a different century, just as introducing the words The Peloponnesian Wars or World War I

can pull you into a discrete flow of time assigned to a displaced fragment…
pelagic, if that's how a particular moment keeps continuing without one being
able to stop it, either around you, in the world, or stuck in the on-goingness of
your mind in a decade preceding you, you trying to pull away from it or it coming
towards you in slow and fast motion. Even as you walk towards the most simple
morning task.

An earlier war could attach itself to the odd assignment of time before
now, not yours, called "Turn-of-the-century," as could the spliced image of a
centaur attach itself to a monster, the new construct borne into overlay as word,
or demonstration of the mind's ability to jump or grasp more than one thing at
a time, this horse/man turning away from or leaving us with its (his?) path of
motion as inadmissible evidence. But also the blur of discrete categories forced
into coupling.

·

Today, walking with you, alongside and then across the Circo Massimo
at an angle down from the upper track and over the grassy slope to the site of
pre-Christian games of prowess and midnight movies in 1983, looking for the
odd bit of archeological evidence, finding an almost buried slab of Roman brick
underfoot, wanting the smaller scale and ordinary blue of the wild flower next to
it. Not as definite as departure. Already it was following the camera's path, its
ability to bunch up time, capture it incrementally or smoothly, into successive
unfoldings, compression fanning out through heat-laminated brick, golden fade-
out into transliteration of…pale fan sent from Tokyo, held in place by a thin loop
of silver paper, just at its breaking point, until the restraint had been lifted away
to release the motion of unfolding. Someone wanting that prop in cultural time.

"May I demonstrate my lineage?"

·

Her feet were already in motion when she placed the fan in a silk brocade box inside another box of smooth cardboard and then a third, of good brown packing stuff, and addressed it to me, smiling to herself while her family awaited her presence at an elaborate dinner staged at the younger sister's house where servants never turned their backs and the chauffeur put his best foot forward for foreign guests—a house in which certain concessions were expected of her, the eldest sister, in spite of her reputation for eccentricities, travel in plastic shoes and the courting of adversity.

What shoes was she wearing, walking up and down hills, looking at our blue water? Her secret was not evident and I could only try to imagine it, even after she told me. Her feet inside and outside of her grandmother's feet, the unbreathing ligaments of even earlier feet in courtly brocade bindings, toes shrunk from the confined pressure of silver loops—the framing of the holding, the plot's single-minded ground—toes now open as a fan to catch light, the unveiled light in her motion away from it.

·

I've understood, too, that writing on a lined page, particularly within the covers of a notebook, has provided me with a landscape of continuous blue horizons, below which I can sink, above which I may again rise, so that each line extended and wrapped into the next enacts a kind of hope, a proof that life below the horizontal does exist and may arise of its own motion or impetus to continue, as in breath, over which we have little control, although we can learn procedures, directing it to foreign anatomical regions.

Today our yoga teacher focused on our feet, showing us how to massage the bottom of one foot and then the other as if it were the palm of a hand, from the center towards the toes with a slow steady upward circling, then directing us to a point below each toe, as it joined the trunk of the foot (if toes were branches), then to bring pressure, followed by an extended pulling and quick snapping motion of each toe. Circulating chi, she said. All of us in a line, doing this.

If you sat in the line of bodies on mats in the yoga studio, under the windows of the far wall facing out to afternoon light just gathering around petals now covering every visible branch (& already shedding on paths), also striking brick apartment buildings behind those trees, but stopping short of the river whose length and reflection must have contributed to the luminous wave and particle motion in the studio, you could feel only half of that light because your back was turned against the source of shifting and pulsing inside the room; whereas if you sat facing the windows, with your back against the opposite wall, as I always tried to do, a different fullness became part of the experience of the room and of the yoga postures as well, a kind of visual presence or figure for the low sound of tablas and stringed instruments coming from a concealed tape deck, as of voices calling after something ahead of them.

My mat was the blue one with my name written at one end, directly onto the foam rubber, in the wide stroke of my teacher's felt-tip pen, and I always looked carefully—once I'd unrolled the mat in the place I'd mentally marked as mine—to find, among the various colored blankets she'd provided in a wall cupboard at one end of the studio, a soft blue plaid that would draw me into a state of calmness, as if the water in the river were also blue, instead of muddy, and the sky an intense wintry cloudless blue, instead of burdening the urban landscape with its heaviness of pale and dark grey storm clouds waiting to break loose…

•

This is what I said about the foot, the man's foot in motion—that is, this is a sentence, once a part of what I wrote down or revised over several days, at least three years ago—this image from another's postcard photo—or it may have been a painting meant to reassemble the accuracy of photography, now both itself, and the fifty word statement I'd prepared for my friends who gathered to share their sentences, limited only by the number of words we'd agreed upon, as if in surprising ourselves skidding into the next arbitrary place, we might extend presence, just as the man's foot—for me, at least—seemed to express a form of desire in the motion of leaving or arriving.

I want to insert the sentence of the foot here but must find where I put it, maybe in a file-folder in the other city where I sometimes keep things—in the cardboard box or the blue plastic vegetable container from the San Cosimato market, left next to the dumpster. But lacking the sentence of that particular man's foot—both its movement, in relation to the wall behind it, and the way it stuck out from the bottom of a trouser leg (which would have been gun metal gray and a sort of late Thirties/mid-Forties cut, because of the WW II dread that seeped into me from it, not thinking about it then but noticing it later, looking back)—I will mark this space as a kind of geometric memory bank, not so much to contain or trap the sentence but to give it a place to rest, once I find it, or even where it might reconstitute itself outside of the context in which it was first discovered.

The sentence, of course, will be different once it has been retrieved. Its placement will change it, but also what has happened to me since writing it may affect my degree of discomfort towards it, so the reserved rectangular box-like container for it might also stand in for something just below the horizon about to rise towards me. But if its substance is represented as that which resides inside the rectangle, isn't it immediately superseded by a symbolic or at least geometric reference to the authority of some earlier contour, even Euclidean in nature? And where does that leave me, I mean, my sentence? When I find it, or even if I simply know that it is in a place where I've stored it, will it still be connected to a pre-existing intelligence network as soft and wet and tangled as any recent technological advance?

•

I must remember to enter the narrator's life in as many ways as possible— by "must," I mean that I crave intimacy and little corners but take even more pleasure in distancing devices, while sniffing the smell of leftover shampoo on a person's damp terrycloth robe. I mean that I want to interrupt with a personal detail. I was stunned, for example, by the exact moment in a recent fictional work when a woman notices her foot stepping up onto a curb and understands this to be an "event." It was not so much the physical presence of the foot. No, that's wrong, it *was* the physical presence (even though we are given no details), but at precisely the same time—as in both sides of an equation—it was her knowing she knew, her discovering for herself the nature of "an event" or that this particular moment, or motion, had any importance at all to her in a world of rain and cars, influenza and the new skin product in its opaque blue glass bottle about to shatter on the edge of the tub, having fallen from the window ledge, a spiritual crisis disguised as diminishing counter space for appliances and other material goods not mentioned.

•

It had happened, had been happening. An incremental shaping, a turning movement. You could also say that something suddenly leapt forward in the dark theatre and that what had been the curb now became a screen with her foot projected onto it just as it was lifting and setting itself back down. The screen was carried inside her, it having already installed itself, forming its contours again and

again, but the light falling on her foot, as it appeared to lift of its own volition—
as a separate animal, even—made it seem as if the projector were also hers,
illuminating the moment which had been gathering in her, yet not hers, until now.

•

(In the middle of this account, the body rises "of its own accord" to
stretch, no yoga class today, no iced drinks, sore throat and every surface feeling
cold against the skin, something obdurate, the nature of early spring, wind and
one's inability to resist it, body over-sensitive, even wrapped in long wool coat.)

At the market, feeling vulnerable in exposed parts, air against face and
hands and grateful for his body guiding me along, across wet rough surfaces,
watching to keep me from slipping, skidding on square stones of little Roman
streets. Man with horse and cart trotting along in traffic. Centaur. My century.
About to turn. The whiff of red tomatoes, still attached to the vine with the same
acrid odor as my father's **V**ictory garden so carefully tended. War stamp days.
Little green beans in the market today, mushrooms stuffed with *con.di.men.ti.*
Behind the flower sheds, next to the iron railing separating the market stalls from
the children's play area, a monster with a man's head and trunk, a horse's body and
legs. His head emits a kind of music, he loves the romantic theme songs of
American movies of the Forties and whistles as he sharpens knives against a device
powered by/turning above a bicycle wheel he pushes, his hooves pressing the
pedals, in place, whistling those old tunes from Mussolini times, but always off-
key. Monstrous to a tuned ear. My ear, my sweet.

Celeste & Sirius

a play for San Francisco Poets Theatre, January 2003

for Eva Hesse, further

Celeste & Sirius

[The setting is Celeste's studio, painting easel positioned backstage, holding a large piece of empty white posterboard, with funky stand next to easel holding several coffee tins filled with brushes and drawing pencils and a bright blue, wide-tip magic marker. A table (or wooden chair) is positioned front stage, facing towards opposite side, holding a small bunch of tulips stuck in a jar; two hats hang from a hatrack]

•

Sirius: [Tapping shoulder of Celeste, whose back is turned towards her easel, her ears covered with headphones to which she listens as she paints. After no response, he taps again...]
Celeste? Celeste... [She takes off her head-phones and looks at him blankly]
Did you notice that the tulips have begun to droop inside their clear plastic jar, even though you pinned and wrapped and skewered them to make them stay up in the water?

Celeste: [Coming slowly out of her interior focus...]
You mean, a bit like a sandwich, with too many things piled inside it to distract you?

Sirius: Not exactly...more like distraction being top-heavy. You know, drooping with possibility?

Celeste: You mean, not as beautiful as that *pure* moment when the perpendicular meets the horizontal? Light and dark pencilled from square to square? [Craning her neck, hand above eyebrows] From here, the tulips are only half-legible, almost resembling us...

Sirius: [Affectionately teasing her]
Re-assembling "Us," again...

Celeste: Well, it seems as if one person's script is always trying to move another person around…or keep you from moving. [Walking back over to the easel] I need to make a statement here: This is *my* canvas because it's empty. These are my newly sharpened pencils and my tubes of paint.

Sirius: You mean they're *yours* because I can see them on the table next to where you're standing, or because *you* just pointed them out?

Celeste: They're mine because I need to stand in a room with a brush or pencil in my hand and feel the paint or the line coming out of me. Did you notice, just as you were talking, how everything changed color, like something with no name for it breaking through you as you were about to throw out the tulips?

Sirius: If you're talking about the purpose of a life, then probably we should put on our hats before continuing. [He looks over at the hatstand, holding their two hats]

Celeste: Because each hat stands in for a part of the mind?

Sirius: I think you mean a part of the *brain*, don't you? [Walks to hatstand, takes his hat and offers it to Celeste] Here's my fedora. Want to borrow it? [Celeste makes a face, declining his offer] Well then, how about your old sun hat? [He hands her the floppy-brimmed straw hat, with a ribbon tied around its crown] We could put them on in unison…and turn on some music. [They both put on their hats and he dances her around as "Chorus of Us" enters, backstage]

Chorus of Us: [3 individuals walking across back of stage in identical attire sing triumphantly]
"We are *Us*, yes we are. We are *Us*…."

Celeste: I've been trying to send you a legible message typed on a standard up-right with slightly blurred letters spilling out over the paper inserted between the typewriter's rubber rollers.

Sirius: Sounds a bit effortful…but I think I see your hand—it could be the Left hand or the Right, right? Perhaps it is reaching into a frayed pocket…the lining is about to go through. [He stops to consider and admire his newly coined image, and then continues] So, here's a thought, as real as your old typewriter. It's going to be alright. We already have a list of words to hold the letters together in a recognizable pattern.

Celeste: [Skeptically…]
Well, we have the history of the Rosetta Stone, too. But what is it, in us, before the words pin us down? I want to find it in the paint or the rope—something we don't understand yet. That would make it better. Then we could both know what we're talking about…or, at least, what I'm *not* talking about.

Sirius: Could "it" be *my* frayed pocket?

Celeste: It could be *the* pocket, before anyone's used it enough to wear it out. [She walks over to the "canvas" propped on the easel and, while speaking, starts drawing a large blue rectangle—meant to represent a pocket—with a wide-nib magic-marker taken from the can. She speaks somewhat slowly as she's drawing] The pocket will be of unsized natural linen, with an upper-case **PKT** in its center, as if hand-embroidered by an Italian tailor….

Now we are living in a different layer of time… [This last, said rather dreamily]

Sirius: [Relieved]
Agreed. Then we'll call the painting "Nostalgia"?

Celeste: …more than that. Whenever *I* paint a picture, it's called at least six things before it's finished. This one, for example, is: "emergency," "curator," "brain tumor," "beautiful corpse," "Shangri-La," "…and, now, the envelope."

Sirius: I hesitate to tell you this, Celeste, but I think you're going down the wrong road—more like a few wrong roads. In fact, I think you're splitting apart at the seams.

Celeste: I suppose you mean that I seem to be unraveling? But *seem*ing may be *my* very important emergency.

Sirius: You're not the *only* one who's urgent. I unpack *my* dog mask often enough—with its long nose adrift—and fit it just over my ears as I move along on all fours through water overflowing and rising around my ankles.

Celeste: You mean that dog is *You,* going forward?

Sirius: [Happy to claim his identity]
You got it. Me, in the water, so to speak. I've been looking at what you're painting and carrying my words between my teeth to rescue you into my perfectly transparent bubble…

Celeste: …words rising out of your little plastic bubble-stick with its ring at the end?

Sirius: That's the way the bubble-stuff comes…inside the jar, available over the counter. It makes me happy to make others happy…well, as long as I know them. Know what they're up to.

Celeste: Their heads seem to turn in unison—as if choreographed—noting each time a new bubble rises and breaks. [Wistfully] We could *all* have jars and stand at the corner in front of the store and blow our bubbles…and stop this worrying. And if a dog swam by, I would know it was You, on your way.

Sirius: [Now less certain, and hoping to change the subject, he puts his hands on her shoulders and speaks to her earnestly]
Let me try a different way of putting it, Celeste…or, to rephrase it: Here's my plan.

Chorus of "Us": [Enters back of stage, with water-wings—or children's plastic or rubber flotation devices—strapped to their shoulders. Each has a card pinned to his/her front, which reads in large letters: HERE'S MY PLAN.]

Celeste: *My* plan is to enter the room carrying a tray with a selection of words, each one inside a long-stemmed wine glass, diverting your attention with my perfectly made-up features.

Sirius: W*ords*? Such as what?

Celeste: Such as words…you know, the ones different people like to say.
[She puts on her head-phones and speaks each word slowly, considering it and preceding it with the word "equals"]

labile=intervention=opacity=dishwasher=discourse=pasta=thermometric bomb=
Top Dog.

Chorus of "Us": [Re-enters with Dog masks, and parades across backstage]
"Bow-wow, bow-wow, bow-wow."

Sirius: A particularly odd kind of music, Celeste…

Celeste: Here, try my headphones…
[She passes them to him]

[Lights down]

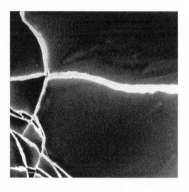

from Fiamma's sketchbook

Hotel Classic

The interior stress of a leaf was forming its own new version
when the hotel came under renovation. Steps led downward
to a drawing of trees, at least in the early draft pinned to his light box.
The architect described in his notes what he thought they wanted,
the clients equal to stargazers or foreign diplomats and wives of
officials from Milano, and he felt that something could happen
on the stairs, an event or motion, as if to rush towards
that noise of the entire tree in stress.

as if we could drink it

In the squeezed apartment, I will find that peaceful island
tempo, still hating the banana peel left on the table,
your thought riddled under quiet of hotel room neglect
and a third (just arrived) confused by three of us instead of four.
Yet often we think of you, how noise of spots on beige pants evolved
the blank page dependency or which line required filing regret.
You try not to make mistakes. The turpentine on your jacket
recedes among bottles (one filled, as if we could drink it).

by heart

dirty bathroom on foreign train, dry rolls in plastic, the woman outside your compartment pulling last night's drummer into her own, you stripping down to essentials of bandage gauze, no lights, *Vouvray* out-flowing under cover of constrained healthy juices, cinema overall restructuring every portion, shepherding the life you've learned by ear, your repetition leader telling you "Alice, we are grown-ups," in public.

loss

You were sitting eating your sandwich between here and
where you'd started from an hour earlier, having abandoned
your overheated car in crosstown traffic,
struck down by an unpredictable wind that slammed through
the pastel threadbare summer. You were off somewhere
attempting to raise a 19th century sail sewn to bamboo stalks with
white canvas leaning & pulling leftward into the watery grid's red edge.

You tried to remember where you'd parked your car. You lifted
the phone to your ear and began: "Oh god forgive me,
I really do like you, but I'm turning back, I just can't keep going on
like this."

Berthe Morisot

Not white. Not the actual resemblance of anything "white" or "pink"
nor its absence, either. Not wayward nor bottled, containing foam
from any excess

observed from triangular pouches rising beneath the ungovernable.

He does not want what he thinks she wants which is to be assembled
from brief measurements of her era's preference, dictated in messages
of convincing urgency arriving almost daily.

Wide puddles of crushed linseed with turpentine added to thin the tobacco-
scented canvas falling from each side of her.

"What is natural?" he asks her—but really asking all of nature, or what
he thinks of as all of nature.

your back to me inside the black suit

Your back to me inside the black suit, inside your back and shoulders fitted into sleeves marked with chalk at the insets. After this discovery, appearing to be exactly identical in intensity to every other part of the backdrop, a person leaning against it as if you,

assigned one full day in which necessity plays its part. Necessary to have a private pink human in the cosmic field: brown window shades delivering glimpses, propelling through to you. (Delete the anxiety of someone's chewing on a word before opening its

pronoun.) What did you mean by the series of inked life stages littering the lower half of a uniformly lined page? Delivering my cool waters rowing through your own personal throat? No need to obscure when a cough can be heard in almost any room—

your precedent for going away. Away is nothing ready for use that has not been preparing itself.

in his white tennis shorts and blue t-shirt

Her father in his white tennis shorts and blue t-shirt—that radiant blue of summer larkspur, he thought—and carrying a racket in his right hand had just imagined hitting a ball to the exact, unreachable corner of the opposite court built within walking distance of the house where her somewhat new husband patiently waited to provide a sort of edge or even to demonstrate his recently agreed-upon worth and he, the father, loped or sprinted out the back door, heading towards the court built on land that extended almost down to the water, free of roads and paths except for those belonging to his neighbors' adjacent land, still a bit wild with ragged spruce—it was possibly the summer before last—and one imagines, not having been there but unable not to think of it, the way a movie scene unexpectedly returns the next morning or even a week or two later, not the entire plot, but often just a moment that repeats—it is in black & white and possibly as short as the length of twenty celluloid frames—and you're surprised that this particular scene should take posssesion of you when the day is sunny and a rather lavish and costly professional landscaping reassures its owner and pleases the Japanese gardener who recently added his own childhood preference for the rock garden he'll cultivate to one side of the back path down near the gate, and her father notices just in that moment that his right leg lifts and he's almost parallel with the new placement of stones, for in my imagining of it the back yard is long and stretches beyond the grey driftwood fence towards a lift of sand and then water so that when she finds him there in mid-body collapse over the back gate, she thinks he might be stretching his hamstrings or resting in an excess of joy, finally alone in the world he's alway wanted.

—for S.G.

perihelion

On her father's shoulders in the Piazza Venezia,
listening to Benito's speeches, with all the men's
and ladies' heads in their winter hats, below her,
and the sun dripping over them

You can hear her breathing
in the photograph

A thief variation: the issue remains unresolved

how a gesture intended as an opening can turn everything in another direction
ruining (without having any idea why) an entire history between two persons at
one time existing in relation, yet in this moment the discovery coming over one,
unprepared for it—sudden piling of dark clouds in the corner of sky, south end
of piazza, sun's light taken from any person sitting with face turned—how, years
later, the impulse arrives similarly to hide or dip below the window, not to be seen

•

hot transfers to cold in company with the narcissist dropping to his knees for
kindling and confirmation

•

Sadi Carnot stood at the edge of reasonable behaviour. I write this sentence
and it invites my scrutiny—the foreigner with her sketchbook, in training

"My name is Sadi."

•

Rudolf C. offers his view, in ink, although Daniel B. in Switzerland has earlier
tried to alert the public mind to the miniscule atoms creasing its facial troughs,
propelled forward through oily pressed heat, film clip after film clip.

•

The issue remains unresolved. In Vienna Ludwig Boltzman stands in readiness
and will not be edited. *Man is not a film* comes over his mind in sentence form,
marching as a dark theory covering the southeast corner of the Platz V. A bowl
of oranges appears—clementines from Valencia—retaining a neighborhood

resemblance. Roundness and orangeness and a bitter oil under the fingernail persist in the face of theory and in spite of a baby crying for attention below Ludwig's window. *The war is our mother, hot goes to cold. we are universal and singular in our direction, tending to heat-equilibrium.*

•

Cold and Hot proclaim their bicameral truths, written as **K** and **H** on the white ceramic tops of water taps protruding from the hotel's bathtub. These would become visible because of the invention of typography, manifest destiny tending toward revelation with the pride of each new intervention and label.

The cars

Sprinting across the freeway just ahead of them having set his left foot down directly onto the pavement from the ledge of the cement divide and edging his other leg forward deliberately—caught the way sports pages show an athlete with muscles condensed in the effort of crossing through a particular space—and then she sees the cars coming towards him giving off that early morning shine across their hoods almost colorless but precipitous in the four-lane parallel rush of metal and cannot tell if any driver straining into the distance further ahead has seen him or possibly has caught that glint off the long black flashlight he appears to carry with its up-beam turned on full and faintly visible due to the angle of early sun falling over the midwestern plains fanning out in every direction away from the sudden view of the airport hub's acclaimed architectural design.

She sees the brief alignment of his body methodically finding its way across the freeway lanes blue baseball cap fit snugly over his head to just above the hairline where now dusky skin of his neck breaks into the picture. *He's made it halfway,* she thinks, but she can't stop the cars rushing towards him even as he scans with concentration the worn lanes for the thing he's lost as if he's walking through the dark and shining his flashlight wherever the object might have landed, his right knee still lifting purposefully upward and forward.

— for C.W.

You can hear her breathing in the photograph

What causes a person—say, in a family—to feel he or she is different from the other members, separate, an extra bit of jigsaw puzzle with unreliable hump, listing to one side of the table after the entire cardboard picture lies perfect and flat?

Who, finally, complies and merges—at every point—with the agreed upon shape of a human torso or preferred community type? Is arrival focused by admirable intention or by an off-camera genetic predictor, trapped just at the periphery of departure? Perhaps it is more like the snapping back of a stretched rubber band to its inherent ovoid design? (Even now I see my current favorite—wide, flat and intensely violet in color—resisting an equal force designed to hold three stems of broccoli in place, pulling away from and then returning to its familiar elastic function closing in around them.)

And what of disruption, departure...even from something that lodges so functionally within one's grasp?

•

For instance, these opening lines—led by grammar and punctuation into the promise of coherence. Now I must turn my back on them. Is it the turning away that marks me? Is everyone else in my "family" looking inward to a center, or are they also turning their gaze sideways? Do they see the gray animal shadow whizzing along the floorboards? Do they hear the parquet geometry of the wooden floor expanding, as if giving-up an hour of footsteps randomly wandering backwards, forwards?

•

Daphne is rushing into leaves. Her mouth is stretching sideways into the opposite of an expanded, purposeful plan. Bernini's chisel lingers inside Apollo's right foot; he's finally coaxed the marble of the left leg into a sprint, showing veins breaking through. But Daphne's traveling ahead of herself. *Why must the photograph of the two of them come out of its envelope every year and be pinned to the wallpaper?* A. still believes D. is the girl he thought she was and continues describing her to herself, even as tree bark is creeping between her thighs and pushing from roots that lift her body higher with the force of minute-by-minute growth.

•

They are two perfect bodies, entirely hard white marble caught in absolute dark. Bernini found the immense hunk of marble, brought down with ropes to the masonry yard near Pietrasanta. A wealthy man paid for the purchase of it, as in gaining on a dream that left nothing in him but a mute feeling-around for something lost—another gamble of horses or dogs contested and persuaded into predatory sport.

Bernini works in marble without knowing what it may deliver. He's in love with the slow revelation of the chase: Apollo's concentration, Daphne's uneasiness. She's disappearing. He knows that much. *Apollo's claim of certainty should be gaining on her, shouldn't it?* You can hear her breathing in the photograph as it's unpinned from the wall and put away in a box, exposing the anatomy of imagined capture, even when you're not looking at it.

•

The museum photographer, noting the Villa's high windows, lights the bodies to catch the dramatic hollows of ribs and male trunk. But it is Daphne's eyes, sliding with the immense pull of gravity, that stop you…you have been taken by the hand and led to this.

Bernini has entered them. The photographer is talking to himself and shifts the armature of high-wattage lighting. *Apollo almost has her,* he thinks. *You can tell by his floating, unclenched hand and the conviction in his eyes as deep and particular as oxygen entering cell walls. He needs—what?—to stop her and to hold the thing he knows must be his, even though some part of him back there in the dark—and because of tracking her inside and outside of time—notices the tough green leaves, probably a kind of tree he doesn't recognize as local, and he's only now seen that they're sprouting, and not just from her hands.*

•

She did not think—or did she?—running towards herself and having no idea of where the next life might be. Out of sight seemed the place.

She was inside and outside of him and visible, forced too soon by his definiteness.

Her indefiniteness was not tolerable to his practiced will.

She wanted the shape of a lintel.

When Bernini chipped the final piece of stone from the block of marble, he saw what he'd done. But it was too late and he'd already turned away.

—for E.B.

Human values

Ascorbate heart tracks every third word, even as bass chords support
the life you imagine ahead of you.

One day or the next day Magellan arrives without limes.

You learned everything from him and rejected it—his right hand wavering above
his forehead made all of us suspicious.

Over white tectonic ivories, a person's body wears unevenly and he is you,
unevenly stressed.

Is that why the average heart weighs less than a pound?

Applause is equal to a sign but it may be canned and fool you, even so pumping
gallons for you.

Arteries appear to carry every third word softly, as if mindfully
inflicting the body's rule.

Loud vessel-wall friction maintains and continuously denotes concentration but
may have misplaced some part of you it forgot.

The *intimate* lingers in its demonstration of how silk stumbles into
privacy through contiguous placement, unfolding in the jacket's lining
(to glow and stay) as asteroids move into sight and await their human names.

Just born cells provide a surface of days advancing: looking down, you
see the lining is shredding and rushing away from ownership,
something you meant to teach yourself to remember.

pressure

During the second half of their marriage, her first husband had drawn a window in oil pastels. Its two curtains pulled apart, as if to disclose a stage whose left panel of turquoise both faced and spread away from its violet twin, revealing between them strokes of densely packed persimmon. She often called this shared part "the middle term" or "invented light" or "the sunset, burning in from the distance." She looked at this picture every day, even carrying it to her new house ten years later upon marrying a second man. The window pulled her into an unnamed world; its grainy surface concealing and exposing something unfinished, so that the turquoise curtain, being closer to expected light, became a defined plane beyond which she might retrieve each vagrant thought.

•

In the first house, a woman in black stockings turns her head away from us and rushes into footage, being someone's first wife or it could be his mother on her way to buy a hat with her shoes in motion, probably blurred by their very movement. The father in this picture (or is it their son, grown older?) has lost his train of thought. His right leg is lagging and barely visible, being out of step with his left, the shape of his arm smudged as if with a watery, mud-colored paint.

•

Blood moves sluggishly through each person's veins, waiting to break the contained surface with an uneven mark. Understanding this, she begins to pay attention to her own pulse and to learn the Chinese method of laying two fingers across the inside skin of the wrist at various points, with one's thumb held firmly below to provide support, and it is then she begins to hear a movement forward or, on some days, not to hear it.

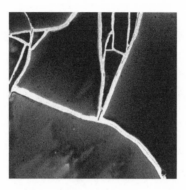

AD notebooks

"…the fear of outliving one's own mind"
—Kenneth Baker, on Willem DeKooning

AD notebooks

notebook 1: Wanderguard

If it has a hallway, I keep it
If it doesn't have a hallway, I keep it

I don't go off She sets off
and comes back and sets off

cloak and hover   sheep together
in hills of plastic   metal

                    hand me   your...

arm/leg how glimmer in milk
their sponge

cleaved clover body   over

now we get our little

        airy cream

      hand me   your…

•

                …they're dyeing me orange…is it the war?
                …when we press orange dye doo-doo into plastic thigh?

     Can't go in or out without
     him   can't get in or
     out can't get
     out   get   out

•

By "the outbreak of the definite" we refer
to tine of fork

         & *won't eat that thing called:*

            (word)   (word)   (word)

sliding over it, pearls glistening chlorine

•

Pink and yellow shine   white passage
exhaled and gone

notebook 2: radiant inklings

She may be tipping from the sidewalk or I'm falling

Cement is under us but grass must leave it
Pink falls, is sanded, flooded, erased and then falls again

I sandpaper my children   My son is at the edge of the sidewalk
and would blot it roughly with a paper towel

"…*because when I'm falling, I'm doing alright…when I'm slipping, I say
hey I'm really slipping most of the time, into that glimpse…*"

When the airplane's flying over the camellia bush

When the airplane is next to the orange tree
it is next to the rose blue pool full of ozone

and I see no one who is me   no body swimming
where I was, who was contained

•

The appearance of his arrival
shimmers but the grasp of it
separates itself from the event

The event's trajectory or possible
history remains athletic but static
You, yourself, may remember a map

in which the colors bear no relation
to the terrain they represent,
the ocean growing lighter & lighter

or its depiction (traced on thin paper)
hangs over it, touching & leaving a smudge.

•

"If the picture has a countenance," he said, "I keep it.
If it hasn't, I throw it out."

•

Yet his desire for her presence remains in him until his arrival at which point she
cannot sit still and must hurry towards a point of light at the other end of the
hallway where they lead him to his brushes and this imagined light he carries in
each step to her door

•

He keeps in a shut paper bag his red and yellow crayons from school
weighting him down which proves the law of usefulness

notebook 3: taking away

She must be

mother light
traded in

for lover light
god in Chicago light

Let there, let there
be word   food   red
& god

every Sunday
borrowing him back

noon's chicken

over them, noodles too &
finally alone

Lead kindly light

I could draw a line with my crayon but the other lines are swallowing it.

then a little humming &
some POP sound pulls sideways
and I'm gone

notebook 4: the erase

he   erases   her
            erasesher

then he

                    takes a little
                        part

      and blows it

                    up p p

as if she
            were
                    floating

      from a string
                        in a scraped patch

or
      corner of

an old Fifties month

                    when then he
                    erased up her body

      which he
      has
      now entirely

                      re-
                      placed

notebook 5: "in spite of gradual deficits"

Through deep parabolas of air you swim up to her.
The room says *I'm a little bit out of this world* but

you are inside her when you paint
and you like the pink embankments of her shoulders

A certain muscular ditch is flawless between two points
You can find both sides of her later

She gives you her colors when you scrape her down and layer her
again with rose madder bleached by repetitions of white in the width of big

embankments, as if you thought of her
as a road to somewhere called "dedication to light"

•

Everything sifts through the painter's torso which is central
in spite of gradual deficits and paired helical filaments,

"like a plasterer laying thin coats of sparkling paste" incised
with charcoal   Turning, staring at nothing, the hand holds

the hard paint tube oozing fresh pigment, stretched & trimmed
Yet her swollen red passages in crystalline absence and array

Drawing from early numbed chatter, trailing bright ridges
of silence   Or the lost year he tried to open her, smearing apart

Again and again pour of turpentine, plaques and tangles
roughly proportional to loss

notebook 6: making more white

takes   little
          blows it   if floating
a string
                    old mouth in   erase
          body   entirely

          parabola air   you swim
                    room says   "this"
but inside her   paint

                              pink   bank   of her

          muscular   between two
can find   sides

                                        scrape her down
with rose   bleached

  in width   if you thought
          a road where   light

               THING SIFTS THROUGH   torso

     spite of   deficit   helical
                    laying thin coats   incised
charcoal   staring

tube oozing   & trimmed
yet   swollen red   absence   array

from numb chatter trail
          silence   lost year open, smearing

               again pour   plaque and tangle
     roughly

notebook 7

the track of DeKooning's hand

                                                    the track of my
                                                    mother's hand

notebook 8

"When you stand among the paintings,"

(I stand among the paintings)

"they make a sharp swerve away"

(I swerve away)

"from what his name attaches to"
"or a leaning into prodigality of"

(leaning, leaning and)

"pink and yellow hallways empty
of the highly composed"

(empty)

"misogynist greens we've come
to know and"

(not, know)

"brushwork gives way to
bounded forms that appear to"

(appear to)

"be drawn and filled in as if
mannerizing his own flesh"

(her flesh)

"exhaled and gone"

(gone)

notebook 9

Disappearing lines on snow.

Pulling his stroke along the dark

granular table. Grains of going away.

Frequently dragging dust into white,

thereby folding himself into her

and leaving her.

NOTE: This poem is for Willem DeKooning and Marjorie Fraser, stricken
by Alzheimer's Disease [AD] in parallel time. Quoted passages are from
Willem DeKooning, Robert Stores and Kenneth Baker.

Photo: A. K. Bierman

KATHLEEN FRASER's sixteen books include her recent chapbook of collaged wall pieces *hi dde violeth i dde violet* and an essay collection *Translating the Unspeakable, Poetry and the Innovative Necessity*. She has collaborated on two artist books—*boundayr*, with aquatints by Sam Francis, and *from a text*, with original paintings by Mary Ann Hayden. Fraser currently teaches a Master's seminar at CCA focused on mixed genre writing and mixed media collaborations. During her teaching career at San Francisco State University she founded The American Poetry Archives and wrote/narrated the hour video "Women Working in Literature." After a Guggenheim took her to Italy in 1981, she established residence in Rome where she and husband A.K. Bierman live each spring, lecturing and translating. Fraser published and edited the ground-breaking journal *HOW(ever)* from 1983 to 1991, forwarding the dialogue between scholarship and innovative writing by women; in 1997 she initiated its more recent electronic version *How2*.

Also by Kathleen Fraser

hi dde violeth i dde violet
20th Century
Soft Pages [pamphlet]
Banners : Tokyo [pamphlet]
il cuore : the heart / Selected Poems 1970-1995
WING
    [letterpress, drawings by David Marshall]
when new time folds up
Notes preceding trust
Something (even human voices) in the foreground, a lake
    [drawings by JoAnn Ugolini]
New Shoes
Magritte Series
What I Want
Little notes to you, from Lucas St.
In defiance of the rains
Change of Address

ESSAYS
Translating the Unspeakable, Poetry and the Innovative Necessity

COLLABORATIONS
boundayr [Limited edition letter press, with original aquatints by Sam Francis]
from a text [Limited edition, with original paintings by Mary Ann Hayden]

OTHER POETRY TITLES FROM APOGEE PRESS

Rules of the House
by Tsering Wangmo Dhompa

"A lovely explication of 'dharma'—things as they are and
how precious they are." —Anne Waldman

bk of (h)rs
by Pattie McCarthy

"This is simply a gorgeous book." —Cole Swensen

fine
by Stefanie Marlis

"An etymology of our sexual and physical lives, our unknown
lives, our daily lives." —Edward Kleinschmidt Mayes

Human Forest
by Denise Newman

"Like imbibing a divine elixir, making one realize how thirsty one
has been all this time." —Gillian Conoley

Apprehend
by Elizabeth Robinson

"I feel a securing confidence in her poems—as if she had
given me her hand." —Robert Creeley

The Pleasures of C
by Edward Smallfield

"These are poems of thrilling uneasiness and probing reward."
—Kathleen Fraser

Oh
by Cole Swensen

"Oh is opera cool." —Marjorie Perloff

dust and conscience
by Truong Tran

"Something extremely important is going on,
something wonderful." —Lyn Hejinian

TO ORDER OR FOR MORE INFORMATION GO TO
WWW.APOGEEPRESS.COM